Fear and Joy
in a Magic Dog

Sharon Waters

*For those who have loved a dog
forever in their hearts*

Fear and Joy in a Magic Dog

by Sharon Waters

ISBN: 978-0-578-91751-1

https://www.facebook.com/sharon.waters.5205

First Edition, 2021

Cover painting of Magic by Janet King

Table of Contents

Fear and Joy
in a Magic Dog

Magic pictures online at
https://www.facebook.com/sharon.waters.5205
Choose: Photos
Album: Fear and Joy in a Magic Dog

In a Cage Far Away

Her bright black eyes sparkled. Spring-loaded with energy, her paws planted firmly on my chest, she beckoned me to play. It was 3 a.m.

Cricket was my introduction to the Schipperke breed. They're characterized as mischievous, intelligent, inquisitive, alert, lively and intense. They're a small Belgian dog that appeared in the early 16th century. Often described as a spitz-type canine, they've performed the herding duties of a Border Collie as well as that of ratter, guard dog and loyal family pet.

It's rumored that when the Belgians were invaded hundreds of years ago, the occupiers disapproved of the locals keeping large, protective dogs and were determined to banish them. In response, the Belgians retained all the attributes of their large dogs, with their talents and courage, by breeding them to create a smaller dog that became the Schipperke. The result is a dynamic canine able to do anything its larger predecessor could perform and then some.

There are few duties they can't manage—when they feel like it. They see themselves as smarter than anyone else, including other dogs and their owners, and their willfulness is a problem for the inexperienced. They're renowned for staring down their people, not coming when called and pretty much doing as they please. They have a high opinion of their own skills and senses, and may fail to obey humans they believe to be less perceptive. Often they're right. I knew a fishermen crew who swore their crewmate Schip sensed through fog more accurately than radar and, poised at the bow, would alert them to any collision danger. They never had a mishap with their Schipperke on lookout.

They're so skilled at guarding people and territory, particularly on boats, that it's said Schipperke translates as "little captain." The name might also mean "little shepherd," since they'll round up a group of anything that suits their fancy

—various livestock, other dogs or kids. These big-hearted caretakers in a small body can live an unusually long time for a dog—up to twenty years and sometimes even beyond that.

With such a high opinion of themselves and a mischievous spirit, Schipperkes are frequently described as naughty. They involve themselves in every activity, affectionately known as schippervising, and can show disapproval with "the stink eye" directed at their person. They will stare intensely at their owners until getting what they want whether it's toys, activities, food or affection. They demand to be included and in the spotlight if something is happening—or if owners would rather rest. There's no time off for their people. There's a caveat that Schipperkes aren't a good fit for those unfamiliar with the breed or unprepared to accept their unrelenting need for stimulation and affection. They aren't part-time dogs for part-time owners.

Advice to think carefully before acquiring one limits Schipperke ownership to those who don't mind turning their lives over to a dog. But for those who choose to spend their lives with these LBDs (little black devils as they are fondly known), the bond is extraordinary. Schips and their people are equally devoted to one another, leading to exceptional rewards for both. Those who own a Schipperke have a common bond as well, since they feel owners of other breeds don't fully grasp how remarkable their dogs are and why they would sacrifice so much for them.

I don't know of any other dog breed that's funnier, with such a quirky sense of humor. However, when Cricket landed on me at 3 a.m., this had been a nightly occurrence for weeks. It was puppy stuff, but with Schipperkes, everything is on steroids and I questioned my ability to keep up with her manic behavior. I communicated with online Schipperke groups, and it struck me that many people had several Schips, some up to four or more. That must be the answer—another Schipperke to absorb Cricket's energy. I would have two wonderful Schipperkes and no problems.

It had taken a year to find Cricket, and she came by plane from South Dakota via a four-hour stopover in Houston. The trip took the better part of a day and she was dehydrated and exhausted by the time I picked her up at Logan Airport in Boston. After seeing her condition, I was determined that no matter where I found my next Schipperke, I'd personally escort the pup to my home.

The Internet was still new without endless chats and infinite interest groups, but I came across a discussion about a batch of Schipperkes in Arizona. The topic was about how to price a kennel of dogs left by a breeder who had entered a home for dementia patients.

While the discussion carried on, I contacted the unfortunate breeder's son, Derek, and said I'd fly out to choose and hopefully take one, a puppy, as a companion for Cricket. I booked a flight to Phoenix for the next week.

My first look at the fifteen dogs in a small, single outside run convinced me that the ailing breeder had been unaware of how much the conditions had deteriorated and the animals had been neglected for some time. I guessed the dogs' situation declined in parallel to the breeder's failing health. Since his mom's departure to the nursing home, Derek had been stopping by every other day to deposit a meager ration of dried dog food and water in the pen. The resulting melee to grab food left the smaller, younger dogs with little left over or open to attack if they competed with the older dogs. Those advertised as "puppies" appeared closer to a year old.

The parent dogs boasted show winner pedigrees, but the paperwork was in disarray and it was anyone's guess which offspring had which parents. That aside, Derek hoped for a financial windfall and had been pursuing Schipperke pricing suggestions through the discussion with breeders. They'd neglected to ask if these dogs were healthy, properly identified with papers and well-socialized—none of which they were. I arranged to stay an extra day to help sort this out.

Unused to the company of humans, the pasal of dogs wandered indifferently around the enclosure. It was clear that some were too ill to go anywhere, and it wouldn't have been fair to Cricket to introduce another dog so sick that it shortchanged the attention I owed her. And any dog newcomer would have to cope with her dominance—would it remind him of being bullied in that pen? I faced a tough decision.

Derek expected that I'd point out my choice through the wire, but I needed more familiarity with each member of this motley pack. Ordinarily, one would expect to be mobbed by dogs hoping to get noticed. Instead, some ignored me while others acted suspicious and kept their distance.

The instinctive bond between dog and human wasn't there. Instead, they were restless and paced like captives in a zoo, ignoring onlookers while preoccupied with their life in confinement. I asked to enter and placed myself in the middle of the kennel, sat down, and told Derek that I'd be there for a while.

Nothing changed. My presence went mostly unnoticed by the dogs swirling in circles as if they were fish in a tank with nowhere to go. I stayed still, making no gesture toward any of them.

Little happened for about twenty minutes. Then I noticed movement in one of the corners. A fuzzy head appeared as if it had grown out of the dirt and a small dog peeked out of his hiding place, a hole he'd dug in the compact dirt of the kennel floor. He was the only dog looking at me. I caught his eyes, and we appraised each other while he struggled to extricate himself from his makeshift sanctuary.

He'd spent most of his life crouched in this hole, so had conformed to the shape of his rough shelter. His unwavering gaze fixed on me as he clawed for a grip on the dirt. The other dogs, tired of their pacing, rested in corners as he summoned the will to leave his refuge and made his way toward me.

He was barely able to crab-walk, but he locked on to me as his destination. With effort and courage, he closed the distance between us and then, without hesitation, settled in my lap. He offered no greeting, but collapsed quietly like a person lost at sea who'd just reached shore. He'd made his decision—he was sticking with me.

He was physically and socially damaged, but his craving for connection overcame whatever terrors he'd endured. Despite lacking much more in his favor, I could work with his resolve to create a bond between us. This would be my dog—we had chosen each other.

My hand traced his body, exploring the thinness, determining the extent of tendon damage. His face was shrunken for a young pup—I guessed him to be about nine months old. His rehabilitation would be demanding, but he was under my care now. I rested my hand on him and whispered that I'd protect him from all harm and that I'd always be near. I kept that promise, my hand always close, shielding him from memories, from real or imaginary harm. I picked him up and he left that enclosure for the first time in his life.

To his credit, Derek was attempting to do the right thing, but he didn't know where to begin. I explained that we had to take all fifteen dogs to the vet, since so many were showing signs of illness. Also, they needed certificates of health from a vet before they could board transport to prospective owners. At first Derek was reluctant to consider flying them to new homes, but they were in more danger here with their illnesses and lack of attention. I encouraged him to concentrate on finding suitable owners anywhere, not the selling price.

We loaded cages crowded with the fifteen dogs into the bed of his truck and headed for the veterinary clinic. After cursory exams, eight were proclaimed too afflicted with respiratory or other sickness to be cleared for airline travel. Fortunately, my little guy was weak, but not infected, so I could fly him home. I wondered if his nightly burial in that hole had protected him from freezing temperatures and pulmonary disease.

The trip to the vet was an eye-opener for Derek, who now realized the dogs weren't necessarily an economic windfall. They were sick, malnourished, and short on socialization. He'd have to cast a wide net for the right owners and lower prices to compensate for the state of their health. I offered $100 for the one I'd chosen. Eventually, I'd move heaven and earth for that dog.

That evening, Derek slid open the glass doors to the yard, assuming I'd put him out with the others, but no way would I abandon my charge to the chilly desert night. He slept with me, my arm cuddled around a dog that had experienced a full dinner without competition, a human friend and a bed for the first time. He gave a shudder and curled up with me. He accepted that I was his defender, but from then on bit everyone else. My new companion had a mountain of fear aggression to overcome.

Getting to Know You

After two days in Phoenix, I was ready to bring my new Schipperke home. I'd come prepared with a pet carrier and had vet papers stating his fitness for air travel. At takeoff, I placed his soft carrier under the seat in front of me, but put my hand through an opening to reassure him as the plane rattled and roared to life. I kept my hand in the carrier until we took off, and then he spent the rest of the trip in the carrier on my lap. As we settled into the hours-long flight to the East Coast, he never fussed, whined, or barked. And so we began our relationship, each of us determined to defend the other from the real, the imaginary and all the phantoms from his past.

He was going to Salem, Massachusetts, the abode of witches and all things mystical. I confided in him that his life would be magical from now on and that his name, Black Magic, signified a turn for the better in an enlightened community known for welcoming those that didn't

13

fit neatly into conventional communities. Magic was fortunate to embark on his new life in this tolerant place.

It puzzled me that Magic trusted me instantly, enough that he crawled over to introduce himself and never misinterpreted my purpose. His world had been a hole to hide in. In his experience, dogs were harmful and humans appeared infrequently—they were distant and unknown. I arrived in his enclosure from a foreign universe and with no introduction, and yet he immediately gave me the benefit of the doubt.

What was Magic's vision from the hole he cowered in? From his panicked reaction to fast movements or anything coming from behind or higher than his short stature, I guessed that attack from above was his biggest fear. If you're living in a shallow hole, everything is above you and any dog in that cage was ready to take a bite out of another. Although he had good intentions, Derek's haphazard feeding routine encouraged aggressive competition and fights. When food arrived, it meant another battle for survival every time. The boundary of his world was a ten-by-fifteen-foot enclosure filled with adversaries. A move toward sporadically provided kibble incited them to attack from overhead—a blur of angry black fur, growls and teeth. Large, dark forms hurtling toward him signaled something that became deeply entrenched in his psyche—that he was about to be pummeled.

I guessed that mostly what he saw was hazy. When I met him, his weepy eyes were encrusted with the ubiquitous red dust of the desert. Over time, the grit had likely scratched his eyes and diminished his eyesight, although I was uncertain how much. Since he startled at shadows, I figured that he lived in a shadow-world where even a boulder we passed on our trail walks appeared as a large dog, hunched over and ready to ambush the unwary.

Of the two things I knew about him, his fear of harm was one. But when he first approached me, I discovered his ability to take a risk and hope for the best. I'd work with that, and Salem was the ideal place.

Black Magic was named for the transformation he would need. His name conjured

up an enchanted life, miraculous and mysterious—
a far cry from his life crammed into a hole in the
Arizona desert. I introduced him as Black Magic
for a while and then just Magic. He was always
magical to me, a creature of exceptional heart,
quirky humor, steadfast loyalty and gallant
bravery. His name was prophetic.

Dog trainers offer tips for introducing a new
dog to your pack. A popular notion is that the
resident dog will resent the newcomer in the home
space, so they should be introduced in neutral
territory where protectiveness isn't an issue. My
theory is that dogs usually enjoy others of their
kind, although resentment and hostility can surface
when it sinks in that the new dog isn't just visiting.
Eventually most dogs will accept that for better or
worse, there's an addition to the pack and will
adjust.

But Magic wasn't the usual puppy. He was
terrified. He froze. His instinct was to prepare to
be slaughtered. But if I sat close, my hand resting
reassuringly on his back, he'd accept the scrutiny
of Cricket. She wasn't impressed. She'd met lots
of dogs, and to her, this one was nothing special.

Cricket had enjoyed a routine where socialization erupted at 5 p.m. every day when neighborhood dog owners gathered at the Salem Common with their canine pals. The dog participants looked forward to the rally so that by late afternoon they were twirling on their leashes to be off to the park and join in chaotic play with their twenty-five or so friends. They were remarkably good. None of them ran off, fought each other or bothered the humans. It was dog time, and park visitors enjoyed the show.

Eventually, the wild meet-up for dogs was banned, but until then, Cricket was queen of the dog party. She was the sharpest, fastest, most agile one of the lot, regardless of size or breed. She was affectionately known at that time as "the Biggest Dog in Salem."

Given her worldly status and Magic's terrified shyness, Cricket didn't take to him. She tried to instigate some play, but there was a bit of bullying in her manner. She'd put on her best impression of a monster dog coming to taunt the opponent. This amused the park dogs, who were confident around each other, but Magic shrank in horror. Cricket looked disgusted, and ultimately decided she'd ignore him altogether.

Magic required special handling when meeting both dogs and humans. I could never assume it would occur amicably without oversight and probably intervention. Left to his own interpretations, he'd bite.

Most dogs work out their relationships naturally, but when introducing humans, there are few gems of advice I came to regret more than "Put out your hand so the dog can smell you." It was a disastrous way to meet Magic. We know that dogs have a thousand times better olfactory sense than we do. So, if we can ascertain who hasn't taken a bath, a dog doesn't need an extended hand to catch your scent. And meanwhile, they're watching and interpreting every move and gesture a human makes.

In turn, body language is a dead giveaway about how a dog feels about you. I don't extend my hand to a dog that's backing away, appears nervous (as Magic usually did), shows his teeth or is growling. My scent isn't going to change the animal's mind, although my posture just might. It's what made all the difference to Magic.

Bending over a dog to extend a hand is an aggressive move to a frightened, intimidated dog. It's been suggested that it triggers a prehistoric response to the leaping attack of larger predators. The bigger you are, the worse it is, and if you're prone to making large gestures or have a booming voice, it exacerbates the perceived threat. For Magic, I'm sure it reminded him of being attacked by dogs in that cage.

When dogs unfamiliar with each other meet, they might roll onto their backs, feet in the air, or freeze with laid-back ears. These body postures mean "I'm submissive, no harm here" or "I think I'll bite your head off." Their bearing is a signal of intent. There's the familiar "play bow" displayed by especially friendly dogs that want to have fun immediately. Shy, timid dogs will shrink backwards indicating they prefer another dog—or you—to keep your distance. And if a dog is unusually quiet, possibly he's waiting for you to get close enough to bite.

In short, most well-socialized dogs recognize

an extended hand as a potential pat, regardless of your smell. They may politely sniff you, but your body language has already passed the test. But if you ignore signals of fear and resulting hostility, an extended hand could be in for trouble. I had my work cut out for me. Cricket was particularly sensitive and forgiving of human social fumbles, but if I didn't get there fast enough, Magic was ready to nip any extended hand in self defense.

Flashbacks

I perfected an encounter sequence when I
was out with the dogs. Cricket handled herself
while I evaluated the threat level for Magic.
Women, calm people and those who spoke baby
talk when greeting him fared best. People who
shouted or used flailing gestures were at risk with
Magic, especially if they moved in too fast to "let
him smell me." I'd drop to my knees to be at
Magic's level, reassuring him and blocking hands
too quickly or roughly offered. My intervention
was necessary throughout his entire life.

Magic tried hard to overcome his fears, and
eventually developed a routine of his own. If he
felt threatened by a too-aggressive encounter (and
I couldn't react fast enough), he'd nip and then, in
almost the same motion, beg forgiveness from the
startled person who didn't see it coming. With
licks and offered paws—and he truly was sorry for
his mistake—he was usually pardoned, but he
couldn't overcome the impulse to snap first.

I'd watch him growl and snap in his sleep and know he was fighting his early battles, crouched down in his hole or dashing to grab a bite of food before he was assaulted. While his new life tempered and calmed that core of his being, the anxiety was always there, and I devoted myself to intervening every time it surfaced.

I interceded successfully most of the time, but sometimes I couldn't head off a bite fast enough. Eventually, I replaced "He had a rough beginning, so don't put your hand out and . . . " to a shortened, "He bites!" I hated to label him as a biter, but it prevented people's instinct to immediately touch him and his impulse to strike back. As in our first meeting, Magic preferred to initiate the approach.

Fear aggression is a particularly difficult behavior to manage and the standard discipline rules don't apply to rescues. Punishing abused, fearful dogs only reinforces their belief that harm comes out of nowhere for no reason—that the world is a hostile place. They don't associate punishment with their bad behavior—instead, it reinforces previous negative experiences. Rehabilitating a dog with fear aggression requires understanding and a lot of patience.

While dropping off a homeless cat at a shelter, I witnessed the sad return of a rescue dog —one that never should have been placed in that home. The teenage girl was in hysterics, sobbing as she handed the leash back to the shelter worker. On the other end of the leash was a large, powerfully built bully dog. He looked docile and friendly enough at the moment, but after three months of getting comfortable in his new home, he'd attacked and seriously harmed the teenager's visiting friend. The dog, at first intimidated in unfamiliar surroundings, had grown confident and protective of his new home and people. Or maybe he just erupted over a wrong move from the friend. It's not hard to imagine that the excited squealing of teenagers might have been interpreted as screaming in distress or aggression.

Choosing Magic, a Schipperke, had a couple of advantages. He was only ten pounds, not the near eighty pounds of the returned bully dog. He suffered social problems, but his desire to engage and willingness to make amends when he erred was a saving grace. Just about everyone in Salem understood, forgave and accommodated his need for reassurance first when meeting him. And he had a devoted champion who'd focus her life on his welfare.

I'm tolerant of animal behavior that doesn't align neatly with human expectations. I appreciate that the wild ones, the "exotics", those other than the traditional dog and cat pets, act in their own self-interest, depending on how they interpret human actions. If cornered, non-domesticated animals are likely to act defensively. They're scared and they don't want to be hurt, caged, or—in their minds—what's for dinner. They aren't nasty, and certainly not deceptive. Their behavior is a straightforward response to fear. Reducing that fear was the solution. Patiently adjusting Magic's world view of others, human or beast, would be essential.

Rehabilitation

Although Magic stuck to me like glue, anyone else was suspect, and in his opinion, likely dangerous or at best indifferent. He'd never had it any other way, caged in with larger dogs competing for food and a human who never intervened. I needed to convince him that he needn't be defensive at every encounter. But for starters, Magic was malnourished and disabled. Beginning with the physical, I fed him the standard dog crummies, but included whole meat —chicken, ground beef, and liver—that I cooked for both the dogs. Even though his jaws were weak, he consumed vast quantities as he made up for lost meals.

But the sight of food triggered his memory of kibble tossed into his cage and being assaulted if he competed for it. When bowls got filled, he'd bolt behind chairs or hide in a corner. He'd approach his meals only if my hand cupped his bowl, reassuring him that I was between him and harm, that he could eat all he wanted unmolested. Then he'd stuff down as much as he could, leaving no morsel uneaten in case he might never be so fortunate again.

I sat next to his bowl, my hand around his bowl, every day for over a year. When I left him with a competent dog-sitter for a few days, he texted a picture of Magic cowering in a corner at feeding time, with the comment that wasn't his behavior bizarre and funny? I explained his fear, but was on my way home immediately.

Magic needed intervention for most situations—feeding, meeting other people and dogs, and doing physical activities. His life spent curled up in a shallow hole caused shortened ligaments and a peculiar crab walk—his hindquarters shifted way to the left as he shuffled along. After he'd been on a decent diet for a few days, I walked the dogs to the pier. The effort of moving through beach sand helped extend tendons and strengthen muscles, as did balancing walks along the top of the uneven stone wall. Daily massage and assisted stretches slowly re-aligned his legs until he gained the semblance of a normal gait, although he forever reminded me of an ambling bear. A year of rehabilitation resulted in his ability to run. Magic was chronically short of breath, although never short of enthusiasm.

The physical rehabilitation took time and patience, but improving Magic's social skills was the most challenging, particularly with kids. Their sudden movements, abrupt gestures and shrieks horrified him. To his mind, ferocious defense was in order. Cautious when introducing him to adults, I worried about his potential with children.

The first time we visited a playground, I knew we were in trouble. Despite his fears, Magic attracted the kids. He was smaller than Cricket, bear-shaped and fuzzy. He and Cricket made an eye-catching pair, but Magic was the one that looked like a stuffed toy. His cuteness drew them in, so I'd have to jump to make sure I could intercept a snap.

We started daily walks that, besides including exercises along the pier, went by a playground at the park. For months we passed it on the other side of the street while Magic, aghast, glared at the antics of youngsters on swings and slides. After months of desensitizing him from his perceived horror, I risked walking him by the children from the closest sidewalk.

I often thought that poor eyesight was part of Magic's problem. I guessed he saw adults as big blurry creatures in motion and children as little blurry beings in hyper-motion. The quick, flailing moves of kids provoked bad memories, whereas the slow movement of adults gave him time to think. I often wondered if, after he made contact with a nip, he realized *"Oh, it's just you, not those vicious phantom dogs."*

To protect kids, I positioned myself at child-level for every encounter. Meanwhile, Magic studied Cricket's behavior and absorbed her solicitous interactions with the little ones. Eventually, it dawned on Magic that these were small humans, and that smaller meant less threatening. He finally accepted that kids weren't frightful demons about to tear him to bits.

Over time, Magic met hundreds of people of all ages. Mostly it was positive once he got the hang of it, although I always dropped to my knees and had my hand ready to intercede in any encounter.

I'm forever grateful to the residents of Salem, who understood and followed my advice on how to approach him. They were patient with his initial growls and tolerant of his tendency to attack shoes. We'd try again, both on our knees, lowered to his level. He learned that people were generally kind and just wanted to meet him. The revelation that people weren't out to kill him gave way to anticipation that they might offer affection, and possibly even a treat. He learned which store clerks had dog snacks, and on our walks he wouldn't allow me to pass by without stopping in.

While I could work with people, it was harder with dogs, especially big dogs. Any dog larger than Magic or that moved beyond wagging its tail, he considered unsafe. I couldn't expect other dogs to be on board with Magic's rehabilitation. Puppies and energetic, lively dogs were a particular challenge that often required us to hurry along. The tragedy was that Magic, more than Cricket, wanted to make friends and play.

Small dogs fascinated him and if reassured, he'd signal a friendly encounter with them by eagerly moving forward with a wiggle instead of backing away.

It was my first experience with owning two dogs, and I learned that they don't necessarily behave according to your plans. Cricket craved wild play with fellow canines. I mistakenly thought a second dog in the house would absorb her excess energy. Instead, I was the one fulfilling Cricket's need for an active playmate, and in addition, Magic's need for reassurance and protection from just about everything. Over the first few months, I recognized that the two dogs might never relate well enough to entertain each other. Instead, I'd be appeasing each of their divergent personalities and needs.

I needed to work out a plan for Cricket and Magic and adjust my own life to accommodate theirs. Instead of one trip to the park in the evening, I undertook two neighborhood walks with them every day.

In the morning, we'd meander along the few

streets to the wharf for Magic's physical rehabilitation exercises. Level strolling on sidewalks wouldn't be enough. At the wharf, I'd guide him along the jumbled stones so he'd use all of his atrophied smaller muscles and stretch constricted sinews. Stiffness and an awkward way of sitting persisted, although eventually, he could keep up with me, if not with Cricket. His strength and agility progressed while Cricket, confident and self-entertaining on her own, hunted for rats lurking in the stone walls.

Later in the day, we'd head for the park where Cricket scintillated as queen of the pack, while Magic, safe at my feet, would watch with astonishment that the savage play didn't end in dog murder.

Magic didn't discriminate—he nipped everybody. His interpretation of anything that moved was that it signaled aggression and imminent harm. And little guy that he was, everything was coming at him from overhead. Just standing over him triggered fear. Worse yet, someone with expressive movements using hands and arms, a person with a booming voice or even the frisky leap of another dog, terrified him. Over the years it got better, but it never disappeared.

I learned to kneel and use a soft voice with baby talk. He moved to nip me only once when I thought he was relaxed enough for a little horseplay. His startled snarl and air snap informed me otherwise. But then as with everyone, he regretted his action and begged forgiveness.

Dogs are far more accommodating of us than we are of them, as we expect them to follow our rules and signals. When unfamiliar dogs meet, they stand still while each gets a chance to size up the other before interacting further. However, humans can be more intimidating with their raised voices and determination to extend a hand and get close. Socialized dogs are used to these greetings and understand that humans have good intentions despite their clumsy introductions. For Magic, every meeting tested his fear level and my ability to manage it.

I committed to inserting myself between Magic and every dog and human he met, every time. Even for people or dogs that he'd come to know. If one walked out of the room and returned five minutes later, it was a fresh encounter and he required repeat assurance. I had to be first at the door, first with every meeting of friendly people on the street or at home. My hand had to be there to intercept, to reassure, to keep Magic from being the dog that bit people. If I could conquer the introductions, Magic was the sweetest dog in the world and begged to be loved.

Besides the walks to the wharf, we'd take leisurely walks around town so Magic acclimated to changing scenery and sounds. After months, I devised a regular stop at the entrance of the downtown pharmacy, which had unusual accordion doors. When we stepped into the entrance, the automatic pleats clanked noisily as they folded open and closed. But as soon as Magic stood quietly in the threshold space, I'd reward the dogs with a treat. Over time, the clamorous thrashing of the doors signaled a treat, and his responses to noisy encounters improved.

In Salem, dogs are welcomed into many of the stores. Bowls of water appear everywhere on hot days. Restaurants with outdoor seating include dog meals on their menus. Residents love their own dogs and enjoy others' canines. I explained to those willing to meet Magic on his terms that a low key-greeting and letting him extend the overtures would work best. I'm still grateful for their contribution to his rehabilitation.

"Rehabilitation" by definition means returning to health. For Magic, his life had been bleak and frightening. There had never been enough food, never a reassuring pat. Cricket was tolerant of him, but was first to the food dish, quickest to dominate attention from humans and dogs, and the possessor of all playthings. What to do? I contacted a highly recommended AKC trainer named Sandy, a woman of keen dog knowledge and a particular understanding of their psyche. I drove Magic over for an evaluation, while leaving Cricket at home.

The session took place in a garage. Without distractions, Sandy and I positioned ourselves in two corners while Magic huddled beneath some shelves. Sandy rolled a ball across the floor. Magic didn't move. He'd never played with a toy and was bewildered as to its purpose. After repeated attempts to engage him, Sandy and I took turns crawling after the ball and tossing it around to each other. Wide-eyed, Magic studied our mysterious behavior. A couple of sessions passed before Magic recognized that he could join in this baffling activity with what he finally understood as a "toy." He was overwhelmed. *"For me? I can have this? I can play too?"*

In another set of sessions for just Cricket, Sandy identified her merits and coached her to pass a Therapy Dogs International exam. She recognized Cricket's sensitivity to human emotions and needs, then led us through the tasks she'd have to learn to qualify. Cricket had to accept that my command was law until I released her, even when I wasn't in the room. I was tasked to hand her over to a child she didn't know and tell her to stay, and then I'd step outside. The goal was to have her remember my command and sit quietly until I returned a few minutes later. Cricket was smart and willing, and passed the qualifying exam on her first try.

This was despite an initial rejection to undergo the test because Schipperkes are a highly active breed often reluctant to take orders. Sandy wrote a letter that convinced the judges to give her a chance, and Cricket performed flawlessly. She went on to do the most amazing work consoling distressed children in a pediatric psych hospital ward. For her, I believe it was less about my commands and more about a job she felt was her calling.

Cricket was a level-headed genius, while Magic was Laurel to Cricket's Hardy, Costello to her Abbott, Gene Wilder to her Richard Pryor. She was the queen, the sophisticated straight man. He was the goof, the jester, the awkward sidekick. I had no idea how to make a team out of this, but Sandy got me there. I signed up for another ten-week session, bringing both dogs together. Sandy did little to nothing with the dogs. Instead, she gave me books to read and proceeded, like a good dog trainer, to instruct and train me.

Sandy revealed that dog life before living with humans revolved around their fears and worries in the wild. Their biggest concern focused on their primary predators—big cats. It became instilled in their subconsciousness to defend themselves against feline-like stealth or outstretched paws with claws extended. It occurred to me that charging up to a dog and thrusting out a hand "so the dog can smell you" mimics that.

For Magic, an outthrust hand offered by a person looming over him sent him back thousands of years, in addition to his early Arizona kennel experience. Eventually, I understood this so well that I reacted instinctively, as he did. *"Here it comes, the outstretched paw—no, don't . . . "* and the reactive snap. I'm amazed at how tolerant most dogs are of human gestures that test their instincts. A scream of delight, outstretched arms, a forward thrust—are a human form of welcoming. Dogs forgive us for this blunder.

Sandy taught me the key to overcoming my reluctance to ask more than would seem reasonable of a dog. "They owe you," she'd say over and over again. "You feed them, house them, care for them. They owe you everything, their very lives, for all the care you give them." Sandy convinced me that "All they have comes from you, so obedience is what they owe you in return. Don't be afraid to rely on it."

As I absorbed her advice, something altered in my voice, attitude and bearing with the dogs. I presumed they owed me good behavior, and they obeyed. It was as simple, and esoteric, as that.

Despite all I'd gained already, I had what seemed like an impossible request of Sandy. Since both dogs were progressing so well, could I possibly get them to follow me on trail walks, off-leash? This is a big ask for Schipperkes. They're notorious for being "runners" and many of them have never been allowed out of the yard without a tether to their owners. If a gate is left open, they run. The drive to explore overpowers any other thought, and they're off.

Getting them to stay with me or in the yard was a challenge, even at home. Cricket would sprint away on a mission if she got out. To my surprise, even though Magic was glued to me most of the time, he was paying more attention to his surroundings than I'd realized. One day I opened a door for a visitor, and quick as a wink, Magic darted down the street. Forget running after a Schipperke. For a small dog, they're fast—really fast. Chasing them confirms in their mind that your mission matches theirs, and they should, if anything, accelerate. I headed for the phone and the Internet and sent the message that a small black dog had gone missing, last seen racing toward downtown Salem.

A half hour went by. The word was out, and a tribe of dog lovers went seeking his whereabouts. Then there was a call with news that Magic had been cornered. He was in a pet store we frequented, happily gorging on dog cookies stored behind the counter. To my astonishment, he had been noting every street to get there on our walks about town and he surely knew where those delicious dog cookies were hidden. I retrieved him and brought him home—several cookies heavier.

Cricket was more sophisticated and better at not getting caught, but both dogs were true to their breed and had a tendency to wander off if given the opportunity to explore. What, I asked Sandy, could I do to get them to follow along on nature trail walks? Sandy explained: "There's your dog's individual personality. Then there's breed characteristics. Behind all that is the basic essence of dog behavior, and you must work with that."

Explaining further, she related the most important caveat: "That will involve trust." Everyone has heard that dogs are pack animals. Although Schipperkes are legendary for inquisitiveness and adventurous behavior, the instinct to stay with their pack trumps all else. Eventually.

A few more sessions with Sandy working on me, not the dogs, and I was ready. I had been instructed to bring along extra-special treats to reinforce the notion that all good things are associated with me and so, armed with treats and trust in the most basic instinct of dogs, I loaded them in the car and headed for the nature reserve. It was an ideal place, an acre or two surrounded by marshes that kept the dogs fairly contained in that area. A multitude of trails with switchbacks weaved along the edge of meadows and climbed up small hillocks tangled with scrub trees. I walked the dogs along the path until we were far from the road and released their leads.

Cricket started off in our usual direction. I stopped and whistled loudly to indicate I was turning down a different path. Cricket grasped my intention right away, and to my amazement, she reversed direction and followed. It wasn't always this easy. Cricket figured she wasn't obligated to follow if she had something more interesting to do. There was the afternoon when I waited a heartbreaking hour for her to show up, although show up she did.

My big worry was she'd catch her harness on something and be stuck where I couldn't find her. If Cricket had a fault, it was in overestimating me. Since she always had a sense of where I was, she assumed I had a similar ability to locate her. On the occasions when she had slipped a branch under her harness and was held captive, she didn't struggle or bark. She'd just wait until I decided she was in trouble and eventually found and rescued her. This was agonizing on several occasions. Just wandering? Stuck with a branch under her harness? Where was she?

To double the worry, there was Magic. His strategy was to rely on others, and either he was on my heels or following Cricket. He couldn't keep up with her and if she wandered far (that would be anywhere out of my sight), he'd be lost. I invested in a professional dog whistle, although after a while I could almost match its intensity with my own whistle. I religiously rewarded dried liver treats to the dog that came when called.

I never chased after either dog. Their responsibility was to "come" and I insisted on it. I'd have never believed it possible without Sandy's instruction, but imperfect as it sometimes was, chasing them never would have worked. The years of happy, free-running walks on nature trails unfolded before us. The off-leash rambles at the nature reserve gave Cricket the freedom for endless investigation and Magic the exercise and activity he so desperately needed while he gained confidence in the process.

Magic discovered a special activity that held no interest for Cricket—swimming. As he put on weight—eventually a bit too much weight—he evolved into a buoyant little fellow. Be it in the ocean or still water, he was always up for a swim. Since my house was only two blocks from the shore, I bought a small rowboat. On calmer days, I'd ferry them out to one of the tiny islands offshore so they could explore as they wished, but it was essential they be able to manage an unexpected plunge into cold and choppy sea water.

Life jackets to fit them were in order, along with training sessions at the beach. With a dog under each arm, I'd wade out neck-high, then release them into the water. The drill was for them to follow me as I headed for shore. They caught on quickly, and I had confidence they'd manage if we landed in the drink someday. The life-saving exercise went well until on one swim back, I heard frantic splashing behind me. Magic had managed to hook his lower jaw under the life vest so that it pulled his face under the water. (How could he have managed that?) I quickly extricated him, but learned that nothing with the dogs, especially Magic, was fail-safe. Cricket with her clever mind could avoid most trouble, but Magic was a disaster magnet.

At the recommendation of a friend, I read a New York Times bestseller about dogs. Basing his knowledge of all dogs on his one canine, the author described them as creatures operating at a limbic system level. They reacted to sleep, food, and walks—but not much else was in their mental toolbox as far as he observed. His dog existed on a leash directed by the owner and couldn't be expected to reverse a tangle around a tree. He wasn't describing a Schipperke, a Border Collie or I'm sure a multitude of other clever dogs.

Cricket always understood the hazard of getting tangled around other objects when on leash. Magic never did—his entire strategy when in any difficulty was to whine, sulk, or just look devastated until Mom sorted it out. My take is that dogs have the breadth of understanding and personality that humans do.

As for abstract reasoning, there was the daily event of the late-night dog snack. The crackle of the bag alerted them both to the impending treat. Magic was at my feet in an instant. Cricket, on the other hand, dashed upstairs and jumped on the bed. She knew that it was where the treats would be dispensed as we situated for the evening, not in the kitchen. Cricket was going to be first because she reached the treat station first—not where the treats were, but where they'd be distributed. Perhaps the author of the book on dog behavior hadn't noticed the cleverness in his furry pal, or maybe his pup wasn't an Einstein, although many dogs are.

Joy

A year passed. Magic was stronger and more confident. He was less nervous about what might happen to him when food was offered, although sometimes I still needed to cup my hand around his bowl for him to feel he could indulge without consequences. His mobility improved, and he walked more steadily. I'd sworn to protect him from any harm, real or imagined and he trusted that I'd keep him safe. We could pass a play yard filled with shrieking children without a meltdown.

Magic idolized Cricket as the big sister. Clearly, she considered him inferior and mostly ignored him, but Magic, besides keeping me in sight at all times, studied her every move. He stayed at home when Cricket visited the kids in the hospital, but occasionally we'd stop by the ladies' elder home. After a year, I decided that Magic should come along. He was stunned the first time I harnessed him up for an elder home visit.

His anxiety that resulted in a nip or a nervous growl had diminished. It was time to see what he could handle, and the ladies were the perfect audience. Their voices were subdued, their motions slight. Being fragile, not a single lady jumped out of her chair to meet him.

To be included was amazing. Like his introduction to toys, Magic was dumbfounded as to what to do. I kept him by my side as Cricket made the rounds in her insightful way. In the hospital, Cricket allowed each child to choose his own approach to her and waited; but with the ladies, she understood that they would remain seated. With no instruction from me, she visited each octogenarian, one after another, lingering just long enough for admiration and a pat. Magic's eyes were riveted to her.

By the next visit, Magic showed his first spark of pure joy. The ladies stayed in their chairs and made no sudden moves. Their soft-spoken words soothed rather than alarmed him. Long ago mothers of small children, they bestowed sweet baby talk on the dogs. Magic made the rounds with Cricket. Gentle hands rubbed an ear, caressed his head. He was astonished and elated that he was included and admired.

Then he did what he would do for every other future achievement, no matter how minor. He came racing back to me, eyes shining, and spun in circles of delight. He had to tell me about it, to report his success and revel in the achievement. In what another dog would have taken for granted, Magic rejoiced. The little black dog positively glowed.

I'm bewildered why any animal behaviorist would find it necessary to test the self-awareness of a dog. Why would it even be questioned? Magic, who reckoned he was a target for anything that breathed, had discovered that he could wander among these seniors and be welcomed, admired and loved. He catapulted into unfathomable bliss. *"Me, Magic, they love me, I'm amazing!"* was reflected in his every gesture on that visit. He was in wonderment as to how his life could have taken such a turn. I had witnessed a miracle.

I can't help thinking that besides being accepted, he recognized that he was being helpful.

He could give as well as he received—he was of value. Cricket possessed a legendary ability to console and comfort with her presence. Magic caught on and reminded me of a little kid chanting, "*I help too! I help you!*"

I monitored Magic's change, but was unaware of how being his constant protector transformed me. I considered his needs before my own. I didn't take a step without him. If I stood, he sat on my foot. If I shifted in bed, he moved closer. More than my shadow, he was nearer than a second skin. His fears infected me, as did his joy. For everyone we met, I instantly slipped down to his side while reassuring him. My hand was a sliver of a second between either a good meeting or a bite. As uncertain as he was at every introduction, few dogs wanted to be loved as much as Magic.

Magic was so close at all times that I'd miss him if I looked behind me more than a few feet. He was close, almost touching, even around the house. For him to be outside without me was unthinkable. He'd made it to the dog store and cookies, but had raced along roads jammed with traffic the whole way. He must not get loose to fend on his own—certainly, no one else could approach him without consequences. On walks, I kept to his awkward, halting pace, the best he could do with his stiffened legs and labored breathing. I absorbed every nuance of his being and identified as Magic's guardian.

Cricket was well known through her work at the hospital. She was queen of the park, the fastest pup, the biggest dog in Salem. She was the polar opposite of Magic's shyness. She was regal and controlled. Magic, always behind, studied her every move from the shelter of my presence. If he managed an engagement that went well, he beamed. If his flashbacks signaled a threat, he bit.

With no regrets, I modified my life around the dogs, especially Magic, as my "special child." I only frequented places that allowed the dogs, such as a dress shop where salespeople would bring outfits to me in the fitting room while they held the dogs' leashes. In the summer, outdoor seating at restaurants and coffee houses offered dishes prepared for your canine companion. It says a lot for Salem that when Massachusetts state legislators passed a "no dogs in restaurants" law, residents gleefully ignored the dictate in outside seating while city officials looked the other way.

I patronized the businesses and other places that allowed dogs (or ignored their presence) and avoided those that didn't. Short stops such as the post office could be managed with the dogs in the car. I left them to bark at passersby while I picked up a few groceries and on rare occasions would leave them at home to visit an art exhibit or go to a movie. But excursions that didn't include the dogs were few and far between.

Nestled along the north shore of Boston, Salem was surrounded by a warren of soggy swamplands and waterways seeking to empty into the sea. Small parks and wildlife reservations where dogs could run dotted the landscape. These were our sanctuaries. Cricket hunted to her heart's content and Magic reveled in the miracle of his unfolding world.

But play continued to baffle Magic. He showed a slight interest in toys, but playing with Cricket wasn't going to happen. She considered

Magic socially too far beneath her and Magic still regarded just about any meeting with another dog as threatening. To give him a chance at canine friendship, I made the error of taking him to an enclosed dog park.

Many Schipperke owners avoid taking their dogs to enclosures dedicated to dog socializing. Schipperkes are a class unto themselves, ready to join a pack of their own kind but can be wary of other breeds. They're guard dogs and may eye new acquaintances with suspicion or hostility. Generally, they prefer human company to interactions beyond the boundaries of their household pack, particularly in confined areas.

I should have guessed it wouldn't go well when I released Cricket and Magic into the fenced area. Several large dogs of various breeds were involved in a rowdy scramble. Cricket was put off and headed for a corner. Magic took a few steps into the middle of the enclosure and froze in terror. His panic drew the attention of the raucous mob and they surrounded him. I dove for him as the first jaw nearly missed clamping down on his little body. The rest I don't remember.

Maybe it was a few seconds, or minutes, before I found myself huddled by the entrance, clinging to Magic and surrounded by concerned dog owners "Are you all right? Are you okay?" I gathered up Cricket and thought I was. When I got home, I discovered a small cut to my lip, but no other bodily damage from the encounter. Although I wouldn't take the dogs there again, I figured we'd survived it. But the next morning, I didn't wake up.

My companion at the time discovered me still in bed, unconscious, long after I should have been down for breakfast. A quick call to the doctor's office alerted them to my condition and that I was on my way. Twenty minutes later, my eyes blinked open. This time I was surrounded by concerned medical professionals. They administered injections of antibiotics and sent me home with more to take until I'd recovered from the sepsis, a result of the dog bite. I decided to stay away from dog parks. I'd have done it again and given my life to protect Magic, but avoiding them was the better option.

Magic returned the favor and avoided the mischief that other dogs usually dispense. His thinking was "*I never do anything to bother Mom. I stick with Mom.*" He never chewed up a slipper, ripped up rolls of toilet paper, destroyed a random mitten fallen to the floor or dug a hole in the garden. If I left him, he never spent time looking for what he could get into around the house.

He'd sit motionless by the door, waiting for my return. He greeted my arrival with an exuberance akin to receiving a stay of execution. He'd bury his head into me, then fall on his back and wail his grief at my absence and overwhelming relief at my homecoming. He made it understood that he thought of nothing but me and that my absence distressed him to no end. This awareness had me hurrying home from even the shortest trip without him.

On edge if caught in long check-out lines or behind chatty patrons, I felt I'd be justified in shouting, "The dogs are waiting! Magic is grieving!" although, I refrained from being a disturbance.

Magic operated on a simple, straightforward philosophy: "*I be with Mom and all is good. All people and dogs are suspicious except Cricket. Cricket is bossy but I know her. All other people or dogs make me nervous. I bite first to let you know you shouldn't hurt me. Then I love you if Mom says you okay.*" Magic healed in some respects but never deviated beyond this.

He was endlessly leery about a new meet, even if you left the room to visit the bathroom and came back a few minutes later. Trivial comings and goings required repeat introductions—even if a person moved to a different chair. He was accused of a short memory—as in only a few seconds—since the reassuring reintroduction was needed after such a short time. Fortunately, most people accepted his quirky behavior.

There was one exception for Magic when it came to meeting other dogs. That was Juliette, one of a pair of long-haired Chihuahuas named Romeo and Juliette. He met her in the pet store we frequented and where he'd run when he escaped to stuff himself with dog cookies. She was tiny and fluffy—beautiful, demure and likewise enthralled with Magic. Magic was smitten. He approached Juliette, body wiggling in delight, while a demure Juliette advanced shyly. She almost seemed to blush. Cricket, completely ignoring them, explored other parts of the store, while a disapproving Romeo barely endured the joyous antics of Magic and Juliette racing around the shop.

We encountered the Chihuahua pair on occasion as, stuffed in small carrying packs, they were toted about Salem by their owner. Magic always thrilled at a glimpse of her. With huge brown eyes and a sweet face, she was indeed adorable. But their owner moved from Salem some time later, and we didn't encounter them again. For years, Magic examined every Chihuahua we met in hopes it might be Juliette—might she be his long-lost love?

But despite Magic having identified the love of his life, I planned a wedding for Cricket and Magic. For Cricket it was another day on the job. For Magic, since miracles never ceased in his new life, the world had come out to adore him. Weddings for people's dogs were popular at the time—pictures and videos of these events populated Facebook dog interest groups and dog wedding articles littered the feel-good pages of local newspapers.

It started from a conversation with the owner of the pet store and she was all in. Jenn would create the outfits for a Cricket and Magic nuptials celebration on the local beach. The wedding attire came together over numerous fitting sessions with the dogs. Cricket wore a satin dress with a three-foot train, tiny flowers and ladybugs adoring the yard of shimmering cloth that trailed behind her. A ruffled Elizabethan collar substituted for a head veil, which Cricket refused. Magic sported the best satin tuxedo available for a small dog. With a matching boutonniere, he was elegantly dressed for the occasion.

It was a community event. The news of the impending wedding circulated about town and everyone was invited. A local green witch—also a legally ordained minister—would perform the ceremony. I arranged for a video photographer, music, a table for the dog wedding cake, and a dog walker friend to escort Cricket down the path to the beach. The guests arrived with dogs dressed in their best for the occasion. A reception followed for the celebratory couple and the canine attendees shared a cake made just for them.

As the beach reception wound down, I took the dogs home for a freshen-up before the limo arrived. Yes, the limo. We had been offered a bridal suite at the local Hawthorn Hotel, a popular destination for honeymooners. Cricket and Magic were taking it all in stride. The hotel lobby was crowded with a human wedding party on this perfect summer day and, still dressed in their marriage finery, Cricket and Magic fit right in. The bemused wedding couple suggested that Cricket and Magic join them for photographs. Pictured somewhere in a wedding album, there's a couple with two little black dogs, also dressed as wedding partners, at their feet.

The day ended with us spending the night in the bridal suite. Room service delivered specially prepared dog dinners while Cricket and Magic tore open gifts of toys and dog paraphernalia. They played with plush bones embroidered with the hotel insignia, as did every other dog welcomed along with their owners at the Hawthorne. Salem was a dog-centric little city united in the fun.

The dog wedding, therapy visits at the hospital for Cricket and the elder home trips for both elevated Cricket and Magic to celebrity status. In our walks about town, it wasn't unusual for tourists to stop us and ask, "Are those the famous little black dogs?" They were.

Magic learned from Cricket that adoration was expected and he reveled in his good fortune. For Cricket, it was like royalty accepting a kiss to the hand. For Magic, the gates of his mental prison flung open. It kept me busy from the second we stepped out the door, kneeling at Magic's side when the dogs attracted attention. For all his joy, the flashbacks were seared into his subconscious— a wrong move could flip his switch. I was never guaranteed an amiable response.

The dogs became good will ambassadors for Salem and local businesses. Their presence was requested for store openings and events, and announcements proclaimed "Cricket and Magic will be attending!" When the Hawthorne Hotel hosted a fashion show to benefit pet rescue, the dogs stepped up when invited to participate as surprise guests. The finale of the show was a couple in wedding dress, since who doesn't love a bride and groom and hosting those events was a Hawthorne specialty. As the human couple started down the walkway, it was announced, "And now, as bride and groom—Cricket and Magic!" By now Cricket was an old trooper at being a celebrity, and I could trust Magic, beaming with confidence, to enjoy himself as he strutted down the runway without biting anyone.

Cricket was such a professional that I didn't notice how sick she was until we finished the walk and were mingling with fans in the lobby. She didn't look good. I hurried her out the back door, Magic in tow, where she vomited up copious amounts of pink emesis. An investigation revealed that, near the lineup area for the runway, a guest had dropped several cold and flu pills. I couldn't guess how many she'd eaten, but I was relieved that she'd regurgitated them and amazed at her professionalism to deal with it off-stage.

I noticed how people greeted and interacted with the dogs in their outfits. The attire signaled they were likely to be friendly and fun. With that in mind, I helped the dogs to acquire a wardrobe for every occasion.

Cricket wore a red skirt with hearts for Valentine's Day, and Magic was decked out in red as well. It's Halloween most of the year in Salem, so they donned several different outfits for the season (which runs from February to December for the Halloween aficionados). My favorites were the bat wings that flopped as the dogs sauntered through downtown. They indeed resembled "bat dogs." For another outfit, long-haired wigs transformed them into werewolves.

When the dogs were in costumes, people smiled and spoke as if they were funny children, and this reassured Magic. It wasn't long before the pair caught on that attire attracted attention and admiration. They couldn't wait to don outfits when dog wear appeared.

Far from having limited understanding, the dogs had senses so acute that I couldn't fathom how they predicted my actions. If I arrived home with a shopping bag containing a garment I'd bought for myself, they didn't react. But if it was dog outfits, they knew before it was out of the bag and they'd be trying to dress themselves.

Dog costumes were expensive, so eventually I found a cheaper approach. I could purchase toddler sizes that fit them—Magic wore size T3, Cricket T4. The cutest thing ever was Magic's T-shirt emblazoned with just "Dance." It suited him perfectly.

Cricket and Magic were Schipperkes of similar age but the similarities diverged when responding to trouble. Cricket was instinctively protective of children. At first, Magic assumed they were aliens from another planet sent to exterminate small dogs. Over time, though, Magic observed Cricket enough that he revised this notion. He observed Cricket insisting on inspecting a woman's bundle brought to the dry cleaners—after all, it might be a child that Cricket needed to look after. She checked kids in carriages and herded wandering toddlers who "escaped" back into their strollers. Mothers were astonished at this dog who assumed a child care role.

Magic learned from her example. Children weren't demons and were often covered with crumbs or melted ice cream he could lick off their clothing. Giggles and hugs weren't lethal—not even painful or dangerous. The kids flailed about more than adults but weren't fast on their feet. Magic's mission with children evolved into a protective role equal to Cricket's, but modified according to his interpretations.

Dogs travel on all fours, while humans are vertical on two feet unless they're in trouble—both dogs assumed that. While the dogs and I were sitting on our porch, we watched a line of toddlers strung together by holding a rope trundle down the sidewalk. But inevitably, the uneven pavement tripped up one tot, who landed face down with a howl. Instantly assuming guardianship, Cricket and Magic jumped to assist the fallen tyke, who was more startled than anything. His human caretaker offered a hug and assurance that he was okay as Cricket dove in with solicitous licks. Magic, assuming that the nearest adult had attacked the youngster and was the reason for his distress, dashed toward her at full charge, growling and ready to bite. I was ready as usual, and intercepted his brave, well-intended but skewed assessment.

Travelin'

I'd had cats when I was working for a sequence of high-tech companies, but I didn't acquire the dogs until after my final layoff in the tech crash of 2001 and moved from Boston to Salem. Working part time in my home business left me time for the extra care the dogs needed. I fit in daily walks around town, hikes at a nature park, socialization with dogs and humans, therapy dog visits, appearances at local events and, especially, my presence during almost all of Magic's waking moments.

Cricket was well-behaved if I left her with others. Magic needed oversight and a willingness to intercede in a split-second when he decided an encounter was a showdown. I had adjusted to his fears and his joys and didn't fully trust others with that burden.

Salem life had been perfect, but cracks appeared in my home life. A twenty-year relationship soured. I drew closer to the dogs for comfort as what I thought was a secure partnership crumbled over that summer. By the fall, I faced the inevitability of a break-up. Staying in my home would be prohibitive on my income alone—its 1730s structure, charming as it was, required expensive upkeep and repair. Just to hang cupboards in the kitchen had cost $20,000 to construct an infrastructure that would hold them. The original house was the simplest of colonials with "two up, two down" rooms and nothing else. The kitchen and bathroom were add-ons. It was barely holding together, and every improvement had to be built to codes that hadn't been dreamed of when it was built.

I would have to move and would need to downsize drastically. I'd packed remnants of my endless projects into every nook and cranny. Items associated with water sports, camping, photography, artwork, vintage collections of every description, books, volunteer programs, and dog outfits were stuffed into closets and corners. Most of it would have to go. If I were to keep the dogs, I'd have to part with nearly all my material things —and keep the dogs I would.

A review of my options with the dogs was concerning. I might, just might, find an apartment that allowed a dog—one dog, not two. A search of private rentals found nothing better. It was rare to find a unit that welcomed any pet. I briefly considered living aboard a boat, but concluded that it would be dangerous for me as a lone person on the ocean and rejected that idea. However, the trend toward RV living seemed a safer and workable solution, so I bought one. To hasten my downsizing efforts, I called an antique dealer, a second hand-merchant, and finally a clean-out guy, and every piece of furniture went.

I had no time to deal with the smaller things individually. I heaped piles of stuff in the driveway, and as the word spread, those hunting for cheap or free treasures arrived to cart their spoils away. I was down to the clothes I thought I'd need, a few cooking utensils, a file folder of paperwork, my computer and the dogs. I hadn't driven an RV before, so pulling off the lot in a 27-footer had my heart racing like an astronaut lifting into outer space. But it was a home for me and the dogs, so I gripped the wheel and drove it the seventy miles back to Salem. I parked in a friend's driveway for the next month while the dogs and I got accustomed to our new home.

I'd hoped to start south in warmer weather. But to make sure I wasn't leaving with health issues, I'd visited the dentist, who pronounced my need for a root canal. Two months later with my dental work completed, I checked the weather forecast and started on a remarkable journey, with two dogs and one cat in tow. The cat, by the way, was Milo and quite a character. His story is in his own little book, not surprisingly called "Milo."

Milo had been with me for several years before the dogs arrived, but he didn't resent their intrusion on his turf. He was mellow and at times almost dog-like as I watched the three of them napping on my bed. He was like a weird dog pal to Cricket and Magic. Cricket defended him from a neighborhood feline that plagued him (Milo was too easy going to stand up for himself) and Magic thought of him as a buddy.

I anticipated that the roar of the diesel engine would freak out Milo, who was prone to drama.

The dogs were regular car passengers, so I didn't predict distress for them, but stocked up on kitty sedatives in case it frightened Milo. But he loved the RV, especially the baskets containing linens, hats, scarves and mittens that he slept in. He took everything about our new traveling home in stride and relaxed immediately regardless of noise.

At the turn of the key, Cricket reacted to the roar of the diesel engine with a yawn. Magic, stunned by the uproar, bolted into my lap and refused to be extracted.

The best decision would have been to crate the dogs in the house compartment and not allow them loose in the driving cabin. I admitted that to myself, but rationalized that riding high in the truck-like driver's seat offered enough protection. Also, I was a cautious driver, traveling on back roads and usually no more than seventy miles a day. Feeling as if I commandeered a well-armored house-hauling tank, I started our slow trek south.

Magic determined that if he was on my lap he'd be safe from whatever was causing the thunderous noise. Cricket didn't care as long as she had prime space in the passenger seat next to me, and Milo slept most of the way. Milo was so unperturbed I figured he'd never need the sedative, so, a few days into our travels, I gave each dog a pill. I hoped Magic would be less apprehensive about the engine noise and that Cricket would be less impatient to arrive at the next stop.

The experiment backfired. After a half hour, the dogs lost all restraint. Instead of becoming drowsy, they snapped to life. They giggled in dog terms, their inhibitions unleashed, while poking at me and each other with delirious abandon. Contrary to my expectations that they'd be calm, they wobbled about like two drunks sharing a hilarious joke. Their uncontrolled levity required me to pull over for the rest of the day, and I chucked the pills.

For our first visit, I drove west for a stop-over with my brother-in-law and his companion. The house was lovely, my hosts gracious. It was an auspicious start until I checked the weather for the following day. The report for January 2nd warned of an impending event, the now infamous Polar Vortex of 2014. The mercury dropped and for the rest of that winter, temperatures fell to unprecedented levels and low thermic records were broken across the United States. My starting delay for dental work had cost me precious time in getting far enough south, although for that winter, anything north of Florida was dangerously impacted by sub-freezing weather.

By February, I was one of the few RVers left on the road. Snowbirds—those who travel to southern states to avoid snow and the worst of winter storms—battled endless days of sub-zero weather instead of experiencing the forty-to-fifty degree temperatures they expected. They weren't equipped for it, and it wasn't fun. Campgrounds closed, while seasoned campers headed for home and their fireplaces. But since there wasn't an apartment to be found for dogs, I stayed with the RV and continued south.

One night my awkward heating system failed —the animals and I woke to find the water in their dishes frozen solid. Milo, unaffected as usual, wasn't unhappy. With his thick coat of long fur framing his face, he looked like an Inuit, at home in the cold. The dogs, however, seemed worried.

Even with their winter jackets wrapped tight, they shivered.

Me being chilled was one thing, but the sight of the frightened, dejected dogs who sensed the world had gone wrong upset me terribly. Feeling responsible for getting them into this frigid disaster, I pulled into a vacant lot and ran the engine until we warmed. Then, I located a gas station with propane for the tanks, filled up, and headed back to the Walmart where we'd parked the night before. I was too exhausted and unnerved to drive further that day.

I needed a fail-safe in case we lost heat again. Leaving the dogs and Milo reasonably comfortable, I walked over to the Walmart and bought armfuls of candles. I lit every one of them that night, and the temperature in the RV's interior hovered above freezing.

There was only one time I was forced to move us into a motel room. Hoping that they'd be quiet enough that management wouldn't suspect my entire menagerie, I moved the animals and plants—every living thing—into our temporary haven from freezing temperatures. Milo howled for an hour before he settled down, while Cricket found a prime spot and slept. As usual, Magic figured if he could nestle with me, he'd be alright.

Despite a rocky start, I traveled with the animals in the RV for three years. Magic blossomed. Since we most often parked in Walmart lots on our travels, with food shopping only a few yards away, separations were few and short. We developed a routine that Cricket enjoyed and that thrilled Magic.

Campgrounds offered little incentive for overnight stops. Hooking up and then extracting systems from their water and sewer services involved time and aggravation. It routinely took twenty minutes with a hair dryer to melt ice and decouple those connections as far south as the Florida border that year. With better WiFi available in Walmart parking lots, as well as having food and emergency supplies close by, we were better off there.

I'd plan the night before, researching the routes and distances and checking weather predictions. Most likely, I'd be pulling into an easily accessible Walmart, right off the highway, from fifty to a hundred miles on, as my destination. And with hard copy notes, I'd have an itinerary prepared even if my computer failed to start up the next morning.

I was never entirely comfortable driving the RV. The view from the cabin, high over the rest of the traffic, instilled confidence, but I never forgot how much weight I was commandeering. It was a relief for all of us when, usually before noon, I'd announce, "Walmart, Walmart!" as we pulled in. Then we'd walk the lot, meeting people who noticed the cute, unusual dogs.

Schipperkes, although small, have a wolf-like profile that makes them striking and distinctive. Since Cricket looked particularly elegant and Magic like a cuddly toy bear, we never failed to attract attention. By now Magic had switched his outlook from "*I'm about to be killed*" to "*I'm adorable.*" Exiting the RV door was like the curtain pulling back as he stepped onto the world stage.

The move to the RV solidified our living as a pack. The dogs decided I had traded the house for the perfect dog den. The bedroom was little more than the dimensions of the full mattress, but with space for everybody—me, two dogs and Milo. The kitchen was only a step away. I never left the dogs to drive off in the car—this was the car—and Magic, plunked on my lap at the turn of the key, was never left behind, unlike the times when Cricket visited the hospital kids without him. We miraculously arrived at a new yard of sorts every day, replacing the previous spot with fresh sights and sounds, unfamiliar smells to investigate and more admirers. Magic felt reassured that, despite the daily transition, our snug little home and my presence were constant.

Magic transformed into a goofball, a character. He smiled noticeably in a wide doggy grin. He was mischievous and appeared to laugh at his version of jokes. He had a wheezy chortle that I swore was a giggle at his own antics. Cricket and I hovered in the background, there to back him up. Feeling confident, he'd exaggerate the delight of meeting friendly people with dramatic gestures and erupt with what I can best describe as a snorting guffaw for his efforts.

Dogs do smile as well as wag their tails. Perhaps because his tail had been docked, Magic poured his thoughts and emotions into his facial expressions more than most. From his look and posture, his state of mind and intentions were clear. I still monitored his encounters with dogs and humans to prevent a nip, but he was generally joyous at even the minor happenings of the day. Breakfast? Delicious. The turnover of the engine to start a new day? *No worry, I'm in Mom's lap.* Arrival at the next Walmart? Ecstatic. A walk over to the Red Box to rent DVDs and meet people? Overjoyed. Meeting admirers around the parking lot? Thrilled. He was truly Magic, wherever we went, or whatever was happening.

Magic was my hero. I could imagine him, a Schipperke Clark Kent, stepping into a phone booth to emerge as Superman in cape and tights, ready to vanquish evil-doers. Most dogs are sensitive to their owner's welfare and state of mind, and none more so than Schipperkes. Relentlessly focused on their humans, they console and comfort, or if need be, head for the rescue.

Being Magic, he interpreted distress on his own terms. Once when vacationing at a lakeside cabin with my older daughter, I spent an afternoon diving in shallow water to remove weeds from a swimming area we wished to clear. I'd surface to hand off gathered weeds to others, then dive again. An increasingly concerned Magic watched from the shore. No longer able to bear his anxiety, he plunged into the water and swam to my rescue, his little head bobbing in the waves. When he reached me, I reassured him I wasn't drowning, and we returned to dry land, to his obvious relief.

His misinterpretations aside, Magic's courage surfaced when it truly mattered. During the years we traveled in the RV, we spent the summers parked at a friend's house in Salem. It was in a lovely peninsula called the Salem Willows, which featured a wild thicket in the interior. It was home to a family of coyotes, more accurately called coywolves since they're a coyote-wolf hybrid and a unique urban dweller. They've lost their fear of humans and frequently dine on domestic pets such as cats and small dogs. The victims' remains, along with collars and tags, can be found scattered about their dens. I was unfamiliar with their habits at the time and mistook one coywolf's interest for curiosity and perhaps even friendliness.

I mistakenly assumed his inquisitiveness was benign, and I'd either ignore the coywolf's presence, or sometimes, pause briefly to return the scrutiny. I was oblivious to the idea that he might be sizing me up, judging how fast I could move or assessing my lack of weapons. The coyote appraised me as an inconsequential human protector accompanied by two little hamburger morsels trudging along behind me. Or rather, Magic was trudging along while Cricket drifted further from my side, darting in and out of bushes after rabbits. The coywolf took each one of us into account, and when Cricket was beyond my reach, he selected her as the easiest target.

This time he didn't show himself while he watched us—he appeared out of nowhere to grab Cricket. She let out a terrified yelp, and I turned to see the coywolf, fangs clamped firmly onto her spine, making off with her into the undergrowth. In the split-second it took me to realize what was happening, Magic burst from his position behind me and exploded into the face of the coywolf like a hand grenade. No matter that the coywolf, at seventy pounds, was a heavyweight to Magic's ten-pound heft. The coywolf spun to confront the valiant assailant, and opening its mouth in astonishment, dropped Cricket. In that second, I moved in to seize both dogs.

The battle didn't end there. With the dogs in my arms, the coywolf followed me home, and having tasted blood, he continued to stalk us for the rest of that summer. He'd be lingering along trails, hiding under porches, or I could see him eyeing us from across the water where coywolves scoured a wild beach looking for carrion. Now that I knew what I was up against, I was able to protect my little dogs. But without Magic's heroic intervention, I'd have lost Cricket that day.

In spite of his internalized fears, when it came to protecting, Magic revealed himself as a courageous, duty-first little guy. Until he'd been assured otherwise, he assumed that a knock at the door was someone coming to steal furniture. He pictured students attending a yoga class on Salem Common, their bodies twisting into odd postures on the ground, as Al-Qaeda militants practicing for their next strike. Size or numbers didn't matter; his mission was to be on constant alert and defense.

In his dreams, Magic twitched and growled, no doubt in pursuit of whatever the enemy was. I imagined him repeating to himself, *"I'm a brave guard dog . . . I'm a brave guard dog."* He surely was.

Small but potent, Magic served as "polite protection." During a brief stop at the corner convenience store (back when I had my car), I'd left the windows open a crack for the dogs to have fresh air. On my return, a disheveled fellow with an equally rumpled-looking companion was peering into the car while the dogs responded to the intrusion with frenzied barking. Intent on examining my car radio, he startled in surprise when I returned. As an explanation for his interest, the fellow remarked that, "My sister might be buying one just like it." Reluctant to make an issue of his suspect curiosity, I waved my hand toward Magic and said, "Just don't put your hand through the window. That dog will bite you." And Magic would have.

The dogs deterred unwanted inspection of the RV as well. It was home, our house, and from Walmart to Walmart, they showed no confusion about our roaming lifestyle. It was the consistent routine that mattered. Our first winter in the RV was a learning experience and test of endurance. Every day took us farther south, but not to warmer weather. Every night was freezing (as were the days) and some evenings, just to break up the pattern, I'd put the dogs in a cart and walk the aisles of Walmart. There were so few people out and about in the frigid temperatures that we had the corridors of foodstuffs and household items to ourselves.

As we crossed the border from Georgia into Florida, we finally spent nights above freezing. I could stop, reconnoiter, and improve our utilities. I had solar panels installed and the heating system upgraded, so we were more comfortable and secure in our traveling den. With our accommodations enhanced, I planned for the trip back north in the spring. I posted ads about my availability for house-and-pet-sitting, stressing that the dogs got along well with other pets and that I had experience with the traditional dogs and cats and in addition farm animals, especially poultry.

One of our first house-sitting jobs required caring for fifty ducks and chickens, plus a soulful Australian Cattle Dog who had breakdowns in the absence of his owner. We were perfect for the task. Cricket and Magic quickly understood that the poultry were to be protected from predators, not chased. Once they learned who was a household member—and each chicken had a name—they patrolled the ground on sentry duties. Before we arrived, a neighborhood fox would frequently invade the flock and kill chickens, but it never happened once on our watch.

The rescue cattle dog, Floyd, spent his early years confined to a single barn stall. The attachment to his human rescuer was intense and he showed extreme distress during their time apart. Given my experience with Magic, I understood, and Magic seemed to also. Magic was a young dog in an old cloak, as was Floyd. They bonded with each other, ambling around the grounds together in, I would guess, mutual ruminations.

Floyd was one of the few canines that Magic befriended. Most dog horseplay reminded him of early experiences with aggression, and he avoided it. He preferred small, gentle or slow-moving pets of any sort. Surprisingly, the guinea hens that screamed in alarm when Cricket and Magic arrived, eventually welcomed him into their cadre as they foraged for bugs around the grounds. Magic identified with their constant search for something edible, and I'd notice him meandering about the lawn in their company. Humped over, searching the grass for anything that hopped or crawled, he almost looked like one of them.

Cricket dominated relationships with other dogs that we cared for, while Magic befriended a few but avoided most. If they were rambunctious, he shied away, never sure if the behavior was friendly or hostile. He was happier with company in pursuit of snacks or sunning in a quiet spot out of the fray.

To fill his socializing needs, I think he ultimately invented an imaginary friend. He'd mock-play with a fake opponent who could do him no harm. Grinning at his own faux drama, he'd give me a sideways glance to make sure I appreciated his silly performances. I played along and cheered his comical antics.

Magic delighted in his heroics, but seemed amused by even his own shortcomings. An example is "snorting," a game of sorts he adopted from Cricket. Feeling satiated after breakfast, Cricket routinely headed for the bedroom and rooted through blankets and pillows, then tossed them all onto the floor. Her sound effects were a distinctive snorting into the heaps of disheveled linen.

Short on breath, Magic mimicked her efforts but managed little more than butting his head and "snorting," a combination of a grunt and a snort, into said pillow. He appeared amused by his spoof of her game and, with a glint in his eye and a giggle of sorts, he'd glance my way to assure himself I was in on the joke.

Magic met his fears and overcame many of them in Salem. During the three-year RV wanderings, he truly experienced delight. Flashbacks could surface, but he had come to expect a friendlier world in those mall parking lots hosting an endless train of Walmart stores down the East Coast. He was a conqueror, a defender, a warrior ready to confront all foes. In his newfound mightiness, he demonstrated a particular humor and elation I hadn't seen in another dog. A prankster, a funny dog who laughed at himself, emerged from the fearful one.

His transformation buoyed me, although I didn't realize how much he'd converted me along with him. I adopted an attitude of "I can do this—I can survive well and live happily in this toy house on wheels." Infused with his delight, I fixated on every move he made, and his joyfulness was mine.

Dogs feel most comfortable in packs, and contemporary advice is for their human owner to assume the role of "pack leader." It implies superiority—the human is the boss, the one who gives direction, barks orders and demands obedience.

But it's only part of the picture. In wild and ancient packs, the leader assumes responsibility for everything. Like a ship's captain, they're on call for any trouble—bad weather, an onslaught, lack of provisions or a plague. Pack members trust that their leaders can handle any challenge to health and safety. The pack leader must be the one who carries a dog under each arm when pursued by the coywolf.

More than just a boss, the pack leader should instill trust and confidence. I was doing well enough as the alpha, but in the process became assimilated into pack life—I felt like one of them. Not that I was a dog, but we were the unit, the team, the gang of three (four with Milo). Their concerns were mine, their fear or anguish, my responsibility to resolve and banish. They needed the pack and, as I became absorbed into their world, I relied on and needed them in turn.

For a few years, it couldn't have been better. The dogs had fresh adventures, new locations to explore and other pets to meet. Moving to a different place every day didn't bother them— home was in the RV, wherever it was. So far it had gone well and the diesel engine was reliable. But what if it suddenly wasn't? The cost of a diesel engine problem would be prohibitive. What if we were stuck on a highway and our little house broke down? How would I explain it to them?

A Magic Life

In our wanderings, I'd imagine each stop as a permanent location, a potential place to set as home. After years of such musing, I decided the South wouldn't work—it was too hot and a plethora of fire ants and alligators, things that sting and bite, were everywhere.

Magic had his run-in with an alligator when we visited a friend at a campground. Always ready for a swim, Magic plunged into a nearby pond so small I doubted it could contain more than a few frogs. Both Magic and I were oblivious to the seven-foot reptile aiming for him like a torpedo. Campers more familiar with the hazards of their locale screamed warnings, and fortunately, I still had a leash attached to Magic and reeled him in before the hungry gator reached his intended prey. I learned to suspect any water, even a soggy drainage ditch along the highway. For a dog that loved to swim, no southern freshwater was safe.

We'd find somewhere up north and manage the winters—hadn't we survived the infamous 2014 Polar Vortex? It would be a relief to be back in our familiar hardwood forests. There were fewer obvious hazards, although the northern woods aren't risk-free.

The RV made it easier to visit friends since I brought my house with me. Needing only a place to park, I was an easy guest. When I wasn't parked with a best friend in Salem, I traveled about New England to catch up with long-time buddies. On a visit to friends in New Hampshire, we shared sumptuous dinners, and my host and I enjoyed trekking through her vast acreage of woods.

Not wanting to impose on them, I spent hours by myself with the dogs in the RV, reading or otherwise staying out of their way. Dinner wouldn't be for at least another hour, so late one afternoon I ventured down a familiar path that my friend and I walked frequently with the dogs. How could I possibly get lost? What could possibly go wrong? I'd been down this trail so many times, and it was a beautiful early fall day. I went just a few yards further than usual and must have taken a slight turn or gone the wrong way around a tree. It doesn't take much to lose one's way, even if you wander just one degree off. From then on, every step was trees and more trees that swallowed up my sense of direction.

Incredulous that I could be lost, I kept going when I should have stopped. Nervous, I wandered even farther into the darkening woodland. Magic trudged along at my heel, and Cricket roamed farther off. Hoping she'd be headed for home, I followed her until I looked up and she was gone. By now, Magic sensed we were off-track and he practically touched the back of my leg as I strayed one way and another. Finally breathless, I did what I should have done in the first place. I stopped, rested, and arranged branches as a makeshift shelter, hoping it would comfort me enough to stay put. But a half hour later as the sun dipped behind the trees, I panicked and started off again.

By now I was frantic. Miscalculating its depth, I walked into a marshy area that might offer a perspective denied me in the thick of the trees. I grabbed Magic to keep him close and out of the wet and weeds. The water reached above my knees as I pressed him against my chest. Maybe it was the cold water that stunned me back to my senses. I turned and went back to shore as the sun disappeared. Back under the trees, it was pitch dark, and I was soaked. The only comfort in the world was Magic, and I held on to him for dear life.

The thick canopy of leaves blocked out any splinter of light left in the moonless night. The dark was featureless—I couldn't make out a tree or a rock. Enveloped in the smell of dampness, I collapsed into the bed of pine needles and moss, Magic clutched close. I didn't choose a resting place; I lay where I dropped. With my face next to the ground, the glow of luminous fungi glimmered out of the black. Sometime during the night, I needed to shift, and in the process I lost touch with Magic. Alarmed, I had no way to find him if he wandered off. But after a few seconds of frantic floundering at the emptiness, I touched him. I held him tight and didn't move again.

Although I was blind and lost in the dark, the mosquitos found us easily. A prick here, a prick there, signaled who they were planning to dine on for their next meal. Magic was restless, and I felt him pawing at his face, no doubt equally assaulted by the annoying, pesky insects. After removing the over shirt I'd tied around my waist, I covered Magic to protect him from the bugs, and at last I felt him sleep. I stayed awake and listened.

A bear, coyotes . . . I'd have no way to see or avoid them in the inkiness. I waited for the crack of a twig, the rustle of leaves, or maybe a grunt or ponderous breathing close by. I'd been keeping vigil over Magic for what I guessed was hours. And where was Cricket? Was she lost in the infinite acres of woodland? Sleep was impossible with the worry.

I wondered what it would be like to sense the first ray of light through the thick woods. Then, so far off it sounded as if it were from a different world, someone called my name.

Clutching Magic, I stood up and yelled for all I was worth. Yes, it was voices, and they'd heard me! It must have taken fifteen minutes for me to understand what they were actually saying as they drew nearer. "The other dog went home, she's fine!" a voice shouted through the dark. More than concern for my own rescue, it was what I needed to know. Relieved, I called back "The other dog is here with me." The dogs were safe.

A pair of lights appeared way off as I talked the Fish and Game team to my side. "Are you okay? Do you need medical assistance? Are you sure? Can you walk half-a-mile back to the road?" I hadn't thought about it, but other than dehydration, I was alright. I could manage the walk back to a logging road half a mile away, and with Magic close behind me, as he had been every step of the way in this misadventure, we reached the truck and drove back to my friend's house.

When Cricket arrived back without me, my friends knew something was wrong. Had I suffered a mishap in the woods? Broken a bone or met a hostile bear? They called search and rescue dispatch, and a highly trained cadre of rescue professionals from the police to the Fish and Game agency turned out. Neighbors joined them to assist, but with daylight waning, everyone except the Fish and Game fellows called off their search for the night. Somehow those two guys guessed where my wandering aimlessly through acres of trees and swamps would take me, and they figured right.

Before they set off for the search, they had asked my friends how I might react to being lost. As a woods-woman, I'd take my predicament in stride, except for the dogs. The dogs were all important, and it was Cricket's arrival home without me that raised the alarm. I'm forever thankful that my first communication with rescuers was reassurance about Cricket and that they understood that fate of the dogs would have been a primary concern for me.

By now it was 3:30 a.m., but the rescue organizers were eager to debrief me. They needed to know the thoughts and reactions of each lost person so they'd be more informed about how the next one might think and behave. After aimless wandering, I'd decided to move toward faint, distant car noise when light returned—there was no doubt a major road in that direction. But no matter what, I wouldn't leave Magic, and they guessed correctly about that. Their instincts and experience in rescue taught them well.

After an hour, the rescue team had the information they wanted and assurance that I had weathered the incident in good health. I closed the door to the RV and slept for a few hours before morning. There was much to discuss over breakfast with my friends. The night in the woods dominated the conversation, but also, I brought up the idea of settling in New Hampshire.

The End of the Road

Three years traveling in the RV with the dogs had been glorious, and I'd do it again. But I worried about how long I could depend on engine reliability. We had endured and survived even the sub-zero weather during the first year. The new heater and solar power I'd installed continued to be dependable, but other systems developed the usual problems of aging in an environment that's constantly rocking along the highway. The water tank had a leak and the electrical features now occasionally went on the blink.

I thought it best to be proactive and so sold my wonderful RV before she developed a serious problem over my budget to repair. My friends suggested an apartment and landlords that would allow the dogs. Reluctantly, I said goodbye to the RV as the salesman drove her away, and we moved into a rustic apartment surrounded by New Hampshire woodlands and miles of stone walls built by pioneer farmers who first tilled the soil.

We encountered dogs and their owners who became our friends. Magic adored our landlady, who supplied him with tasty bones he relished, gnawing them to bits with his few remaining teeth. (His early malnutrition had resulted in premature tooth decay and only a few were left.) No worries for him, he was getting affection and attention wherever we went. He missed Milo, who had died of cancer the year before and was buried in Milo's Meadow near my friend's house, but the dogs were living a carefree life in our rural home.

For me, it was a relief not to worry about technical and logistical issues on a daily basis. We had walks in the woods and amiable landlords. I raised chickens for eggs and Magic enjoyed hanging out with his fowl friends. He had two Pomeranians dog pals that visited, or we went to visit them. With his own territory to defend, Magic reverted to guarding instincts, but challenged few people, and bit fewer still. Maybe only one or two.

Our daily routine adjusted to having a permanent location. In the RV, the first thing was to check all systems and our itinerary. As reliable as the RV engine was, my fingers were crossed that she'd start. Some days it was so cold in the cabin that the GPS wouldn't respond. I'd have to start the engine and hold it near a heat vent until it revived. Driving would be more or less stressful depending on the highway traffic. Every stop at the next location brought relief that we'd made another leg in the journey.

Now in our New Hampshire place, after a quick sip of coffee, I'd don whatever gear matched the weather—summer shoes or winter boots—to release the chickens for the day. Following the morning chores, we'd wander along the trails that crossed through acres of woodland and old colonial fields. It was glorious living for Cricket and Magic. After being lost that night in the woods I was more cautious about taking unknown paths and often carried a compass. Although the dogs ran free, I carried a leash just in case there was a need to keep them close.

And then there was the day I needed to have that leash. It started routinely, with us stepping out onto a path we'd wandered so many times before. It was a delightful early summer day that started peacefully enough, the wind calm, the air dry. Sunlight peeking through leaves stippled the path. Then came the crashing and howling of the dogs as a full-grown black bear bolted across the path, hotly pursued by first Cricket, then Magic right behind. What Magic lacked in speed he made up for in enthusiasm for the chase. Fortunately, the bear didn't guess that these dogs were harmless to him, and kept going until he was out of sight.

What was it about this day? Not far along more barking erupted. I followed the sounds of the ruckus to where the dogs had cornered a pair of coyotes defending their den. Unlike bears, coyotes will kill and eat dogs, especially little ones with overconfidence in their powers. I moved in, snapped both dogs onto the one leash I had and escorted the two self-satisfied rascals home. That was enough adventure for one day.

When called to duty, both dogs responded with courageous enthusiasm. I suspected the reason bears or coyotes never menaced the chickens was due to the dogs' diligence in patrolling the yard. Although bears had attacked our neighbors' chicken coops, they had avoided us.

Coyotes watched the yard, but never dared to threaten the chickens. Regal Cricket took the job seriously, while Magic reminded me of Bert Lahr as the Cowardly Lion in "The Wizard of Oz." His humor included being able to laugh at himself when posing as the unlikely hero.

When he wasn't defending home and hearth, Magic had one toy. Or actually, two favorites but only one at a time. His first attachment was to a small lamb (Lamb Chop) containing a squeaky. Cricket had no use for toys—she wasn't into 'kid stuff for baby dogs.' I'd seen her hog all the toys when we were visiting or pet-sitting, but not as playthings. She'd bury them so no other dog could find and play with them.

But Magic had 'Lammie' and Cricket never touched his possession. He'd chase after Lammie but only a few times, then he was winded and the game was over. Lammie occupied the floor wherever we lived for years, then finally disappeared. I suspected Magic had taken this special toy outside and forgotten where he left it. Without Lammie to comfort him, Magic eventually attached himself to Yellow Fuzzy Ball.

Yellow Fuzzy Ball was about the size of a tennis ball, had bright yellow fur and, of course, a squeaky. If this most desirable of toys had a face when it was manufactured, it quickly went missing. Like with Lammie, Magic would chase YFB if tossed, but Magic had his own way of relating to it. Instead of the usual fetch, he'd imitate its bouncing as he pranced, all four feet leaving the ground in unison each time as Yellow Fuzzy Ball hit the floor and sprang into the air. He expected me to fetch it and repeat the toss so he could mimic its hopping flight across the room. It wasn't the chase that thrilled him, but rather the joy of impersonating each bounce—he didn't play with it as much as he joined with Yellow Fuzzy Ball in it's lively trajectory.

The more attached he grew to this toy, the more Magic worried it would be stolen or lost, the way Lammie had disappeared. He'd be napping, perhaps worrying in a nightmare of a Yellow Fuzzy Ball theft, then startle awake to go searching for it. Once found, he faced the dilemma of where to hide it. He scouted for hiding places in the house but eventually, he decided it was best hidden outside somewhere in the yard. He could spend half an hour sleuthing different locations, tucking the special toy under a bush, behind a gathering of flowers or in a clump of grass. He didn't dig, instead using his nose to push aside dirt and then cover his precious possession. It was never satisfactory. He'd relent, and a few minutes later retrieve it to repeat the process of selecting a hiding place and burying it again. Both dog and toy became filthy in the effort. Magic spent several years absorbed in the process of either bouncing with Yellow Fuzzy Ball, or worrying about how best to hide it from any dog or human who might want to steal this precious treasure.

The welfare of the dogs determined my choice of living space. It was crucial to live in a dog-friendly town with places to take walks and hopefully where the dogs could run free in open spaces. New Hampshire had suited us, but another option in a house owned by my family became available in nearby Vermont. Here was an opportunity to be closer to family, while living in an independent space with a large, fenced-in yard and no restrictions on the dogs. Delighted with this idea, I packed up and we headed for Vermont.

It was perfect. I had neighbors, but not on the other side of shared walls as in apartments or condos. Barking at the door or yowling at a dog three houses down would go unnoticed outside our walls. A short distance away was a nature park with trails. We'd been lucky in our travels but now we were secure in our own dog-friendly home.

We soon found friends when Cricket and Magic met Eddie (named for Thomas Edison) and Little Bear. Their owner, Rachel, and I accompanied the motley canine crew along wooded Vermont footpaths where we met up. The dogs did as dogs do—they inspected each other, then established a social order. Cricket was the leader although she couldn't match Bear's puppy exuberance. Eddie was a happy joiner, while Magic thrilled with any inclusion he was offered. He hung back a bit from the others, sticking close to me while also imagining himself a vital member of the gang.

Cricket, Eddie and Bear absorbed themselves in the exploration of every smell and dashing after scurrying chipmunks or other critters that crossed the path. Magic followed along, elated at joining a dog adventure on a lovely day. Cricket, Eddie and Bear raced far ahead. Magic trudged along with Rachel and me, partly due to his physical limitations and partly because he always had one paw in his own world. Suddenly he stopped and with all four feet tucked under him, sprang straight up, leaping into the air while bouncing in a circle. "What's that about?" asked Rachel, startled by his sudden frolic.

"Magic's joy," I said. "He does that."

No Words

He was twelve and overweight, a result of making up for early food deprivation by gobbling everything. He'd always been slower than other dogs due to his neglected puppyhood, but that summer he slowed even more. On our daily walks at the nature park, I matched my pace to his. His stride shortened, and his steps sometimes faltered. I chose easier paths in case I had to carry him.

As his physical strength declined, he seemed to spend more time in his imagination. There were his spontaneous leaps of delight and his mock play with fantasy friends. Sometimes he gave side glances for assurance that I appreciated his performances, although I guessed sometimes he conjured up an illusionary audience as well. His antics were for my benefit or pure joy, although late one afternoon I watched as he sat in quiet contemplation on the back steps. Like a portly old miniature bear lost in thought, he surveyed everything and nothing in particular.

I sat in a chair inside the porch and watched him. What was he thinking—what did he picture in his mind? Did he remember his early life, cramped in a dug-out hole? I doubted more than a shadow of that existed, surfacing only when he was startled by the unpredictable movement of a human or dog. His little shoulders relaxed. More likely he saw visions of Juliette sitting coyly beside him. Perhaps he remembered his old buddy Floyd ambling after his rescuer as they strolled about the chicken-populated barn and grounds.

He might silently chuckle at the costumes he'd worn to amuse and gain such admiration from humans. Bat wings at Halloween guaranteed smiles. Long hair dragging along instigated hilarity when it was announced he was a werewolf to celebrate the season. But best of all, his toddler-sized "Dance" T-shirt proclaimed him as the funny little guy that he was.

Might the murmur of a diesel engine pulling a truck down the street remind him of the faithful one that carried us thousands of miles up and down the East Coast visiting friends, stopping for weeks at a time for house-sits, or parking overnight at one Walmart after another? While the two of us sat, we listened to the brook gurgling as it meandered among the old willows behind our yard. How many times had he paused for a dip in that cool water under the trees, or gone swimming in a lake or in the ocean? He sat quietly, gazing into his dreams.

Dogs barked in a yard farther down the street. I'm sure he thought, "*I'm on guard, I'm the tough dog here, I've barked at you before!*" When did he transform from the pup bedeviled by cage-mates to the fierce protector who chased a bear? No harm had come to any chicken on his watch—he must be feeling proud of that.

Maybe he just watched for the rabbit to scamper by as it usually did this time of day. A quick dash in its direction with a menacing bark would send the varmint back under the fence. Interrupted in his daydreams, he caught sight of a bird, destined at this moment to flit through the air in front of us and then be gone.

That weekend Magic left me. We'd been out visiting when a stroke took him. He was gone before we made it to the vet.

There are no words. No words. I had barely taken a step without him at my heel for twelve years. At every encounter, I'd gauged Magic's reaction and intervened if necessary to reassure him and safeguard that no one got bit. I felt as if he took me with him—or wished he had. What would a day be like without worrying about his fears and delighting in his spontaneous acts of joy?

His death had pulled on a thread and Cricket unraveled. Retreating into a corner, she neither moved nor made a sound. She tried to greet me at the door with the hysterics that she and Magic shared upon my arrival, but then retreated in confusion as to what had gone so terribly wrong.

I'd lost my mission, the dog that determined my reaction to whatever we encountered. First, I always had to explain Magic. I'd have to convey why this dog, grumbling the equivalent of expletives under his breath, would either bite or adore you, depending on how you projected threat or benevolence in your greeting. Or why the ritual needed to be repeated on every re-entry to a room, even if one had only stepped away for a minute. Everyone's move was Magic-monitored, Magic-accommodated, Magic-focused.

There were no bounds to the hole that Magic's passing left. I didn't think I could recover and Cricket wasn't doing well. We were subdued, withdrawn, unable to console each other. When Magic's ashes arrived they were some comfort, as if some part of him was near. But the hollowness in the days was devastating, and I worried for Cricket.

Magic couldn't be replaced and further chronicling of those days is too wrenching to relate. With such a vacancy in my life and Cricket's perpetual mourning, I decided to fill it with, if not Magic, at least a dog that we could offer a caring home. To this day I don't understand the amazing good fortune to have Schipperke puppy Tonttu arrive at our door. He left us little time to mourn. If Magic had been an awkward angel on earth, Tonttu was the rascal who escaped from the circus.

There was nothing Tonttu couldn't, or wouldn't get into. The vigilance I had centered on Magic transferred to Tonttu in keeping him entertained and out of trouble. Cricket startled away from her grieving and, at Tonttu's insistence, began to play again.

Time passes, and Tonttu is a much beloved fixture in our family, and Cricket and I moved on. We enjoy walks in the park, meeting with dog friends and each other. But Magic will be missed forever, his face grinning out from a portrait a good friend painted of him—that expression of anxiety to trust, hesitancy to bravado, of fear transformed to exuberant joy.

The End

Epilogue

So often I've seen online posts that start like this: "It was ten years ago today that Mika passed..." Then begins the eulogy for a dog that died long ago. The words relate an extraordinary relationship, one that will never cease to be mourned.

We've called our dogs our children, but they never grow up, become independent and leave us. Maybe the relationship is more like a strong marriage, a permanent bond that grows more precious over time.

Dogs don't leave us for someone better, who's younger, prettier, richer, or doesn't do that annoying little thing that you once loved but now hate. They don't lose interest, hold grudges, demand more, lie, or outgrow you. The attachment is unconditional, unrelenting, and permanent.

The relationship with a dog can be

extraordinary and to lose such a friend is indeed heartbreaking. As they loved us so well, we knew and loved them. In time we move on but never forget our days with them. We're forever grateful for the Magic they brought to our lives.

www.ingramcontent.com/pod-product-compliance
Lightning Source LLC
Chambersburg PA
CBHW061743020426
42331CB00006B/1338